A Lion First Guide

Starting with the
New Testament

STEPHEN TRAVIS

A LION BOOK

Text copyright © 1994 Stephen Travis
Illustrations and maps copyright © 1994
    Tony de Saulles
This edition copyright © 1994 Lion Publishing

Published by
Lion Publishing plc
Sandy Lane West, Oxford, England
ISBN 0 7459 2420 4
Albatross Books Pty Ltd
PO Box 320, Sutherland, NSW 2232, Australia
ISBN 0 7324 0780 X

First edition 1994

Acknowledgments
All Scripture quotations in this publication are from the
HOLY BIBLE, NEW INTERNATIONAL VERSION.
Copyright © 1973, 1978, 1984 by International Bible
Society.

A catalogue record for this book is available
from the British Library

Printed and bound in Singapore

Contents

1 What's it all about?   7

2 The story that had to be told   11

3 Headline events from Luke's Gospel   16

4 Same story, different angle: the four Gospels   29

5 Followers of Jesus: the Acts of the Apostles   33

6 'My love to all of you in Christ Jesus': Paul's letters   41

7 Too hot to handle?: the book of Revelation   48

8 A message for today   54

9 A message for me   59

The New Testament
is a book about
Jesus Christ. It is
also a book about
us, our concerns
and questions.

1

What's it all about?

• • • • • • • • • • • • • •

Huddled together under the corrugated iron roof of a *favela* in Rio de Janeiro, twenty people of various ages are talking excitedly about the meaning of the Bible for their lives.

At a university in Siberia, 150 staff and students—most of them not Christians—are studying a passage from the New Testament and asking what it means for them.

In 1991 a man is made Archbishop of Canterbury who, as a teenager, began to go to church and 'found the worship boring but the preaching from the Bible riveting'.

What is it about the New Testament which claims such attention? How can a small book written so long ago still have such influence in the world? Why should it matter to me?

To answer these questions we must go back to Jerusalem in about AD30. Jesus, from the town of Nazareth in the north of Palestine, has gained a reputation as a prophet and miracle-worker. Some Jews have treasured the hope that he will deliver them from

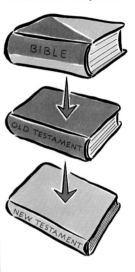

The Christian Bible is divided into two parts:

The word 'testament' means 'agreement'. The Bible's first half is about the agreement God made with the people of Israel, while the second half—the New Testament—revolves around the agreement God made available to all people through the death of Jesus Christ.

7

the occupying armies of Rome. To his closest followers he is 'the Messiah'—the one specially sent to bring God's presence and his blessings close to people in a new way.

But the religious authorities, worried that his popularity may undermine their own position, have joined forces with the Roman governor Pontius Pilate to get rid of him. Pilate has sentenced him to be horribly killed by crucifixion. Jesus' followers as well as his enemies have watched him die, and his body has been taken away for burial.

Now it is Sunday morning, two days after the crucifixion. Some of Jesus' followers come as mourners to his tomb. To their astonishment, they find that the huge stone which sealed the tomb entrance has been rolled away, and the tomb itself is empty. And then Jesus, in a series of appearances over several weeks, shows himself to them unmistakably alive! He has risen from death!

Jesus' resurrection meant for his followers—and means for us—that he is alive for ever, available to bring God close to men and women

The event of that Sunday transformed his followers' lives. Jesus' risen life, his resurrection, meant for them—and means for us—that he is alive for ever and available to bring God close to men and women.

The New Testament is a book about Jesus Christ. Without his resurrection it would not exist. It is also a book about us, our concerns and our questions:

◆ **What is the purpose of life?**

◆ **Is it possible to know God in a personal way?**

◆ **How can we live so as to make a better world for our children?**

◆ **Why am I such a mixture of hopes and failures, idealism and selfishness?**

◆ **Why doesn't God do something about all the suffering in the world?**

> I went to the Commonwealth Games in 1986 in a bit of a turmoil, wondering what life was really about. As I went into the room there was a Good News Bible on my bed. I picked it up and started reading it. I met a character in there I'd never met before, and Jesus Christ challenged me to think about what the real meaning of life was. And I liked the things he had to say. Most importantly he seemed to respect me for who I was as a person, and I was challenged. Nine months later I asked him to make himself more real to me, and my faith grew from there.
>
> Kriss Akabusi, Olympic athlete

The New Testament was written over a period of about fifty years by a variety of different people. In this sense it is a fully human book. The difference is that God chose its writers and inspired them to write in such a way that their words revealed the character and the plans of God.

Through the words of the New Testament, the risen Jesus speaks to us about ourselves and about his purpose for us. But how are we to hear and understand what he says? Where should we begin to read?

The first thing to notice is that the New Testament isn't one book, like a novel or a biography. It's a collection of twenty-seven books, written in different styles by a variety of authors.

And there's no better place to start than with the writings of the man who wrote more pages of the New Testament than anyone else. His name is Luke.

The New Testament isn't one book, like a novel or a biography. It's a collection of twenty-seven books, written in different styles by a variety of authors.

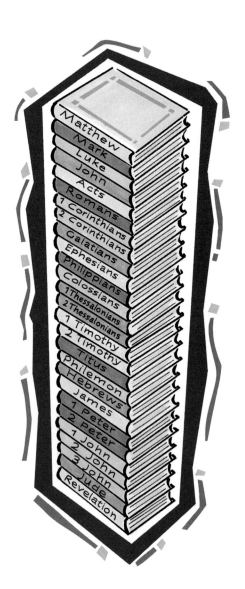

2

The story that had to be told

● ● ● ● ● ● ● ● ● ● ● ● ● ● ● ●

Luke is one of four people in the first-century church—the first people who became followers of Jesus—who wrote 'Gospels'. We tend to think of them as biographies of Jesus. But what strange biographies!

They tell us almost nothing about Jesus' life before he was thirty years old. They don't tell us what he looked like. They tell us very little about his inner thoughts and reasons for doing things. They spend a surprising amount of space on the last week of his life and the circumstances of his death. Why? Because they aren't simply biographies but Gospels! The word 'gospel' means 'good news'.

The Gospels tell the story of Jesus not just to give us interesting facts about a historical person. They tell it so that we may discover good news about how Jesus can make a life-changing impact on us!

This is what makes Luke's book, and the other Gospels, different from any other book. He tells stories about what Jesus did and said in Palestine around AD30

The story of Jesus' life was so dramatic, so life-changing, that his followers made sure that it was recorded.

so that we get an impression of what kind of person Jesus was, and why he had such an amazing effect on people.

But, remember, Luke believes in the risen Jesus—the Jesus who is alive today. So whenever he tells a story about the Jesus who taught and brought fresh hope and healed and forgave people in Palestine, he is saying at the same time that the same Jesus can do the same things for people anywhere, any time.

That's what makes his book good news! That's why we read it today and expect it to affect our lives.

It didn't occur to Jesus' followers to write down an account of his life immediately after his death and resurrection. Most of them were not bookish people. Stories about him were remembered and passed on to others in the course of preaching the new message. Where people don't have books to rely on, their memories remain amazingly vivid and accurate.

But about thirty years after the resurrection, when many of the people who had known Jesus in Palestine

How to find chapter and verse

If you wanted someone to find a particular passage in a modern book such as Graham Greene's novel *Our Man in Havana*, you would simply tell them to look up page 73, or whichever page you have in mind. With the Bible, a method of providing references was devised which can be confusing if you are not used to it.

To make it easy to refer to particular sentences in the Bible, each book is divided into chapters, and each chapter is again divided into verses. So 1 Corinthians 13:4 (or 1 Cor. 13:4) means Paul's first letter to the Corinthian church, chapter 13, verse 4. John 3:16–21 means John's Gospel, chapter 3, verses 16–21. 2 John 12 means the second letter of John, verse 12 (this short letter is not divided into separate chapters).

The contents page of any Bible or New Testament lists the books in the order in which they appear, and shows the page on which each one begins.

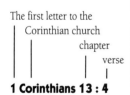

The first letter to the
Corinthian church
chapter
verse
1 Corinthians 13 : 4

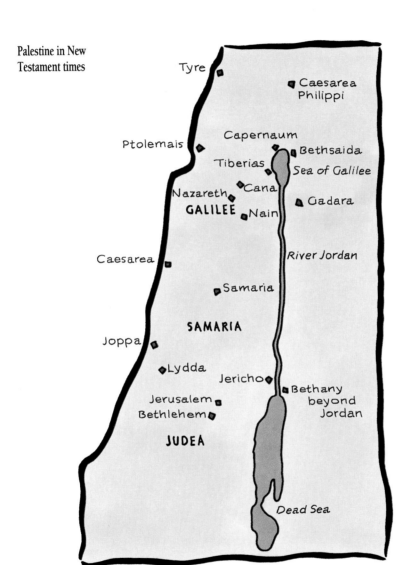

Palestine in New
Testament times

Tyre

Caesarea
Philippi

Capernaum

Ptolemais

Bethsaida

Tiberias

Sea of Galilee

Nazareth Cana

GALILEE Nain

Gadara

Caesarea

River Jordan

Samaria

SAMARIA

Joppa

Lydda

Jericho

Bethany
beyond
Jordan

Jerusalem
Bethlehem

JUDEA

Dead Sea

were at the end of their lives, Christians began to want an accurate written record of his life to pass on to the next generation. One of these writers was a Greek called Luke.

We know little about Luke, except that he was a doctor and a friend of the apostle Paul (see Paul's mention of him in his letter to the Colossians). He is probably the only non-Jewish (Gentile) writer in the New Testament.

Luke wrote two books—the Gospel according to Luke, and the Acts of the Apostles. The second of these we shall come to later, but let's look first at his Gospel.

It will be helpful to have a copy of the New Testament, or of the whole Bible, handy. It is available in various modern translations. I recommend the New International Version or the Good News Bible.

Luke opens with a statement about why he is writing.

Many have undertaken to draw up an account of the things that have been fulfilled among us, just as they were handed down to us by those who from the first were eye-witnesses and servants of the word. Therefore, since I myself have carefully investigated everything from the beginning, it seemed good also to me to write an orderly account for you, most excellent Theophilus, so that you may know the certainty of the things you have been taught.

LUKE 1:1–4

He tells us here that others have already written about Jesus, drawing on the stories constantly used in the church's preaching. He tells us that he himself has done some careful research to check out the story he is about to relate. He dedicates his book to someone called Theophilus, probably a new convert to Christianity, who has promised to meet the cost of producing Luke's two books.

And Luke's purpose in writing is to bring home to Theophilus the 'certainty' or the 'full truth' of what he has so far been taught about Jesus. Naturally, his book has a special attraction for people exploring Christian faith for the first time.

The word 'apostle' comes from the Greek word for 'messenger'. Jesus' closest followers were called his 'apostles' because they spread the message of his resurrection, but Paul became known as 'apostle to the Gentiles' because he told non-Jewish people (Gentiles) about Jesus.

After that he launches into his story. And there's no better way to find out what he says than to read it for yourself. To read it in three manageable sections, I suggest dividing it like this:

◆ **Luke 1:1–9:50**
Jesus' birth and his life and teaching in Galilee

◆ **Luke 9:51–19:27**
Jesus' journey to Jerusalem

◆ **Luke 19:28–24:53**
Jesus' life, death and resurrection in Jerusalem

But to get the flavour of what Luke especially wants to tell us about Jesus, we'll dip into five episodes in his story.

Luke wrote down what he knew about Jesus to tell the 'full truth' to his contemporaries. What he tells is as relevant today as it was all those years ago.

15

3

Headline events from Luke's Gospel

● ● ● ● ● ● ● ● ● ● ● ● ● ●

Luke's Gospel is the story of Jesus told in such a way as to show what his life and teaching, his death and resurrection, can mean both for Luke's first readers and for us. Its message is fresh and relevant after all these years because Jesus himself is as alive now as he was on the first Easter Day.

In five episodes from this story we can get the message of Luke's Gospel—we can find out what sort of person Jesus of Nazareth was and is.

King born in cattle shed!

Read Luke 2:1–20

We'll begin with the familiar story of Jesus' birth. Luke tells this story in a way that emphasizes three things about Jesus:

Jesus was born into a particular place in the world at a particular time in history. His birth in Bethlehem and his life in Galilee demonstrate that God is not remote from our human lives; he is involved with us.

Firstly, **he sets the birth of Jesus in the context of world history**. Augustus, the Roman emperor, controlled Palestine as well as most of Europe and all the countries around the Mediterranean. Some of his subjects called him 'saviour' because he had brought peace and stability after a period of civil wars. But Luke is announcing a different kind of ruler, a different kind of saviour. And this saviour will go on affecting the whole world long after Augustus is forgotten.

Secondly, **he reports the actual birth of Jesus**. The census has made Joseph and Mary return from Nazareth, where they live, to Bethlehem, Joseph's family home. So Jesus is born in the town of his ancestor, King David.

This underlines his role as the *Messiah* (in Greek, *Christos*, Christ) expected by the Jewish people. The Old Testament led them to expect that one day a descendant of David would deliver them from all their enemies and bring in 'the kingdom of God'. Then at last there would be peace, justice and a world living in harmony with God. As we shall see, Jesus does bring the kingdom of God, but not quite in the sense that many Jews expected.

Thirdly, **Jesus' birth is announced to the world**. There are no headlines in the newspaper, no cards in the mail, but a whole chorus of angels. And the receivers of the message are not national and religious leaders, but shepherds.

Why shepherds? Just because they are ordinary people. The good news of Jesus comes first to people who have no religious qualifications, but are open to the possibility of being surprised by God.

Jesus has many titles in the New Testament. A 'saviour' is someone who rescues (or 'saves') people from danger. 'Messiah' is a Hebrew word meaning 'anointed one'. Being anointed with oil was one sign of kingship, and the Jews longed for the leader who would bring in God's kingdom. 'Christ' is the Greek word for Messiah.

Drama in Nazareth

When Jesus was thirty years old God gave him authority to begin preaching in public and healing people. In the synagogue in his home town of Nazareth there occurred one of the most dramatic incidents in the New Testament.

Read Luke 4:14–30

Jesus goes to the local synagogue—the building used for Jewish worship. He is invited to read from the Scriptures. He reads from the prophet Isaiah, a passage which speaks of how God will bring new hope to his people.

Then he makes the startling announcement: 'Today this scripture is fulfilled in your hearing.' What prophets glimpsed from a distance, what God's people longed for, is in their midst as he speaks. The kingdom of God has dawned because Jesus is here.

The passage from Isaiah lists several signs which would indicate the arrival of God's kingdom.

'Today,' says Jesus, 'those things are happening in what I am doing. The kingdom of God is no longer something you hope for in the future. It is something you can experience and be part of now. God has come close to you.'

'Preaching good news to the poor' sums up what Jesus was most concerned about. 'The poor' are the people who are powerless, the people written off by the political and religious establishment, the people who don't count for much in the world's eyes.

In Jesus' time they would include not only people who were short of cash but also widows, orphans, refugees, the disabled. And people who were despised because they did dirty jobs or because they benefited from the Roman occupation of Palestine. Jesus came to show God's love particularly to such people, and Luke wants the world to know about it.

When people respond to Jesus he welcomes them into a new community. Those among his disciples who have been battered by society or by circumstances are accepted and valued in a new way. Those who have been gripped by evil habits are set free by the power of his love. 'Nobodies' become 'somebodies'. Their world is turned upside down.

The Jewish Scriptures are what Christians call the Old Testament. At the synagogue service Jewish men would take turns in reading and explaining the Scriptures.

Key stages on the journey through the New Testament

1 Jesus is born

The place: Bethlehem, a town in Judea, 10km south of Jerusalem.

The event: it's a well-known story — no room at the inn, shepherds, a star, wise men, a baby born in a cattle-stall — it's the story Christmas is made of!

The significance: There would be no New Testament, no Christian faith without the life which began in Bethlehem. (The event was so significant that the world has marked time — AD means after the birth of Jesus — from this event onwards.)

2 Jesus begins his work

The places: Jesus began his work in Judea. But he soon went to Galilee, where he quickly attracted followers. The centre of his activity was Capernaum.

The events: Jesus heals people, he teaches, he gathers a band of twelve followers, his miracles and radical teaching catch attention — not least from the authorities.

The significance: in only three years Jesus caused a real stir — his life and words changed people's lives. He never travelled further than 150km from his home town, but the message he preached has since travelled the entire world and is still changing lives 2,000 years later.

4 The early church grows

The places: the message spreads out from Jerusalem through those who witnessed the amazing events of Jesus' last weeks on earth and through followers such as Paul, who tirelessly and fearlessly declare their beliefs.

The events: persecution of Christians by the Romans, amazing stories of martyrdom, churches growing far and abroad, Christian teaching and practice tested and confirmed.

The significance: the incredible way in which the early followers of Jesus went out and spread the news about his life and teaching is testimony to the strength of their belief in him. It's hard to imagine that they would have gone out, against all the odds, and spread the word if they had had any doubts about his resurrection. That the message is alive today, that there are millions of followers of Jesus the world over, is even greater testimony to the truth of the New Testament story.

3 Put to death and raised to life

The place: Jerusalem, a site called Golgotha

The events: the Sanhedrin (the Jewish Council of Elders) convict Jesus of blasphemy but are powerless to sentence him to death; only the Roman authorities can do that. After some manoeuvring, Pilate, the Roman governor, is persuaded to carry out the sentence. Jesus is hung on a cross, between two thieves. After six hours he is dead, and is placed in a tomb cut out of a rocky hillside. A huge stone seals the entrance.

But three days later the tomb is empty and Jesus appears, alive, to many of his followers. Within two months of Jesus' crucifixion, they are boldly proclaiming that Jesus is alive. They are prepared to suffer – even die – for their beliefs.

The significance: Christianity hangs or falls on the resurrection of Jesus. It is the climax of God's rescue plan for humankind, opening up the way for us through death into eternal life with God. You can't get much more significant than that!

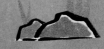

But the episode at Nazareth is not finished. Jesus goes on to remind hearers how it has always been God's plan to show his favour to Gentiles, not just to Jews. Old Testament prophets such as Elijah and Elisha were sent to show God's care to people outside Palestine.

'The kingdom of God has dawned in your midst,' Jesus is saying. 'You can know its blessings—but only if you'll share them with others.'

This is more than the audience can take. They rise in hostility against Jesus, because he has threatened to disturb their cosy assumption that God is more concerned about them than about anyone else.

This story sums up the pattern of Jesus' whole ministry as Luke portrays it. His mission is especially to bring to the poor the good news that they are loved and valued, and to give them new hope. The rest of Luke's Gospel will give examples of Jesus showing God's generosity to all kinds of people who were looked down on by many of his contemporaries—people with leprosy, Samaritans, tax-collectors, those whose sins shocked society.

And his second book, the Acts of the Apostles, will report how the early church reflected Jesus' concern for all such despised people. It will show especially how the church fulfilled God's plan that his love should be made known to Gentiles.

Shocking teaching

No one can respond to Jesus without being changed by him. He makes demands on his followers which stretch their imagination and test their commitment to the limit. Here is one section of his tough, down-to-earth teaching.

Read Luke 6:27–36

To get the full force of what Jesus is driving at we must ask, who did Jesus mean by 'enemies'? To his first

There were many despised groups in first-century Palestine: people with leprosy—not only infectious, but unclean by the Law's standards—tax collectors, who were seen as collaborators with the hated Roman authorities, and prostitutes. Jesus brought new hope to such people by showing them God's love. Today his followers still care about those society would rather forget.

hearers one answer would spring to mind: the Romans. How could anyone be more hated than the foreign dictator and his armies who control your country?

So we can imagine the shock and the anger when Jesus tells people to *love* the Romans. 'That's outrageous,' they say. 'That's the last thing you'll find us doing.'

'No,' Jesus replies. 'Unless we dare to do good to our enemies instead of matching hate with hate, there will never be a new world of peace and trust. We shall destroy ourselves. And remember, if you have entered the kingdom of God you are called to be like God. And he is generous to those who hate him as well as to those who love him.'

Probably when Luke's readers heard the word 'enemies' they would think of people who hate and cause trouble for the Christian community. When we hear it we may think of people who treat us badly or belittle or despise our opinions. To all of us Jesus says: 'Love them, do good to them, pray God's blessing on them. Dare to break the cycle of hatred, and you will be acting as children of God himself.'

That is what Jesus did himself. And where did it get him? To a cruel death on the cross, and his ideals destroyed with him. But the resurrection which followed his death shows that self-giving love always wins in the end.

Innocent man is crucified

This is a long passage, but the central event of the Christian story cannot be rushed.

Read Luke 23:1–56

The stirrings of opposition to Jesus have reached their climax. Jewish leaders have arrested him and have challenged him, 'Are you the Son of God?' But only

23

Pilate, the Roman governor, has authority to condemn a man to death. So to Pilate Jesus is taken.

His accusers try to get Pilate's support for the death sentence by claiming that Jesus is a serious threat to the country's political stability. Pilate is unimpressed by this and regards the case as just a tiresome dispute between religious groups. Herod Antipas, who by Rome's permission ruled over Galilee where Jesus was brought up, taunts Jesus but has no basis for condemning him.

Ironically, Jesus' accusers call for the release of a real terrorist, Barabbas, in order to secure the condemnation of a supposed terrorist, Jesus. And Pilate, to save his own skin, allows himself to be bullied into granting their demand.

So Jesus is led away to one of the most painful forms of execution ever devised. It was reserved by the Romans for slaves, foreigners and particularly violent criminals. He is mocked and humiliated to the end. But those who mock speak truth without knowing it. It is because Jesus refuses to save himself that he is able to save others. Through Jesus giving his life, God's love draws people to himself.

Even as Jesus dies he is calling down forgiveness on his executioners. And bringing hope to a criminal crucified alongside him.

Crucifixion: 'the most wretched of deaths'— Josephus, Jewish historian.

'. . . the very word "cross" should be far removed not only from the person of a Roman citizen but from his thoughts, his eyes and his ears'—Cicero, Roman statesman.

Witnesses confirm Jesus is raised from death!

Jesus' death was like thousands of other deaths in those times. But then something happened which marks him off as unique.

Read Luke 24:1–53

On the Sunday morning after Jesus' death, the shock-waves begin. Women find the tomb's entrance open, and the huge stone which sealed it rolled to one side. And the body of Jesus isn't there!

Has it been stolen? But who would have any reason to steal it? Bewildered, they suddenly see two angels gleaming with heavenly glory.

'Why do you look for the living among the dead?' they ask. 'He is not here. He has been raised to life!'

Even though Jesus has hinted that death would not be the end for him, the women find this too good to be true. And when Jesus' disciples hear their report, they mutter into their beards about hysterical women. The tomb may be empty, but *how*?

The stories of Cleopas and his friend, and of the risen Jesus later meeting his eleven disciples, show how the amazing truth dawned on them. The Jesus who had been dead and buried in the tomb is now alive!

He is not a man restored to earthly life, like someone who revives after lying in a coma. Nor is he a ghost. His earthly body has been raised and changed by God into a form fit for the everlasting life of heaven.

That is why his friends don't immediately recognize him. He isn't merely the same as he was before death. But then his words, his actions remind them of the Jesus they knew so well. So this Jesus, who has shown them more of God than they have ever glimpsed before, will stay with them for ever and share his life with theirs.

Jesus' followers went on to prove that this contact with Jesus was no one-off, peculiar experience. They began to tell the world how the man from Nazareth had opened the way to God. Despite tremendous opposition, they led many people to share their discovery that Jesus is alive and anyone can find him. But Luke needs another book to tell that story—the Acts of the Apostles.

The resurrection of Jesus is the *only* historically recorded event of its kind. It is God's way of saying to the first Christians and to us:

◆ **God's rescue of the human race from sin, a rescue which began way back in the history of the Jewish people, reached its climax in Jesus.**

Sin is the self-centred attitude that deliberately goes against what is right. It damages both ourselves and other people.

'Then they
put him to
death by
nailing him to a
cross. But God
raised him from
death three days
later...'
Acts 10:39,40

'I am the
resurrection
and the life. He
who believes in
me will live,
even though he
dies...'
Jesus' words
recorded in
John 11:25

'But the truth
is that Christ has been raised from
death, as the guarantee that those who
sleep in death will also be raised.'
1 Corinthians 15:20

◆ Jesus has opened the way for us through death into eternal life with God.

◆ God's power which raised Jesus from the grave is available to strengthen us when we live his way and share his love.

Amazing happenings—Jesus disappears!

About six weeks after Jesus rose from death, the appearances which he made to his followers came to an end. Luke's Gospel ends and the Acts of the Apostles begins with the story of Jesus' final appearance and return to God—the ascension.

He spoke to his friends about how they were to receive the power of God's Spirit to enable them to share with others the good news of his resurrection and his love for all people. And then 'he was taken up before their very eyes, and a cloud hid him from their sight'.

We may wonder exactly what kind of event these words are trying to describe. But probably Luke wants to tell us what the event *means* rather than what it looked like.

The ascension **marks the moment when Jesus' work on earth was complete** and he was welcomed to his Father's side as victor over death.

The ascension **prepared the way for the feast of Pentecost**, ten days later, when God would come to his people in a new way.

Because Jesus lived on earth as a human being, his work was restricted to particular times and places. But now that God expresses himself in the world in the form of the Holy Spirit, who filled the apostles at Pentecost, he is at work in all kinds of places and people at all times.

Jesus opened up the way to God for all people by showing us what God is like. His life and death and resurrection show a love so strong that it can even overcome death—a love that can cancel out our wrongdoings.

The ascension means that **Jesus has authority over his church and over his world**. Looking around at the world, we may wonder whether this is so. Evil and conflicts between human beings continue because Jesus does not force people to do his will.

Yet he has set limits to the power of evil. He is working towards his final victory, drawing people under the influence of his love. Christ's ascension points forward to the day when his defeat of evil, suffering and death will be complete and his people will be secure for ever in his presence.

Same story, different angle: the four Gospels

● ● ● ● ● ● ● ● ● ● ● ● ●

You may wonder why four people bothered to write down the same story about the life of Jesus. Wouldn't one have been enough?

But when you want to find out the truth of a story, you go to the different people involved to get their angle on it.

Even eyewitness accounts of an event don't tally exactly—one person sees one detail clearly, someone else will bring out another point. And that's how it is with the four Gospels.

Luke is one of four people who wrote Gospels in the New Testament. Each Gospel-writer tells the story of Jesus in his own special way. Three of the Gospels—Matthew, Mark and Luke—contain material which is very similar. For instance, Jesus' teaching about what is demanded of those who follow him is found in Matthew 16:24–28, Mark 8:34–9:1 and Luke 9:23–27. It looks as though one writer has used another as a source for his own writing.

The Sermon on the Mount contains Jesus' famous teaching on how to be happy (or 'blessed') which turns normal expectations upside down. Mourners will be comforted, the meek will inherit the earth and those who are persecuted for doing right will inherit God's kingdom.

Blessed are the poor in spirit,
for theirs is the kingdom of heaven.

Blessed are those who mourn,
for they will be comforted.

Blessed are the meek,
for they will inherit the earth.

Blessed are those who hunger and thirst
for righteousness,
for they will be filled.

We can't be sure, but it seems most likely that Mark wrote his Gospel, the shortest one, first. Probably he was writing it for the church in Rome at a time of persecution, about AD 65—some thirty or so years after Jesus' death.

He gathered together stories which were familiar from the preaching and teaching of apostles such as Peter, and wrote them in a way which would encourage Christians in Rome as they faced the prospect of suffering for their faith. He emphasizes the sufferings of Jesus, as if to say, 'In your own suffering you are being faithful to your Lord and Master.'

Probably Matthew and Luke later copied parts of Mark and added other teachings of Jesus and stories about him which would particularly express what their readers needed to hear. Both of them included stories of Jesus' birth, which is not in Mark, and further stories about his resurrection.

Matthew added a lot of Jesus' teaching to what he found in Mark. The Sermon on the Mount, for example, gathers together key elements of Jesus' message about how to follow him. And Matthew was also concerned to show the relationship between Jesus and God's promises in the Old Testament made to the Jewish people.

Luke added incidents and teaching which illustrate Jesus' concern for the poor, the outcast and non-Jews. We see this, for example, in the reports of Jesus' first public teaching in the synagogue at his home town of Nazareth.

John's Gospel is rather different. It shows little sign of having been copied from the other three, and contains few of the stories found in them. Its style is more reflective, penetrating to the inner meaning of Jesus' life, death and resurrection.

Its famous beginning shows how the birth of Jesus was not a new thought on God's part, but was the result of God's eternal plan to communicate himself personally to men and women.

The Gospels give us four portraits of Jesus, each stressing some particular aspects of his life and his meaning for us, which together give us a full picture.

MATTHEW portrays Jesus the teacher who fulfils God's promises

MARK portrays Jesus the crucified Messiah

LUKE portrays Jesus the saviour of all

JOHN portrays Jesus the eternal Son of GOD

Jesus is called the Word of God because he is the ultimate way God has chosen to communicate with people—by becoming a human being.

In the beginning was the Word, and the Word was with God, and the Word was God . . . The Word became flesh and made his dwelling among us. We have seen his glory, the glory of the One and Only, who came from the Father, full of grace and truth.

JOHN 1:1, 14

5

Followers of Jesus: the Acts of the Apostles

● ● ● ● ● ● ● ● ● ● ● ● ● ●

If you think the church is dull, inward-looking and living in the past, you should look at the Acts of the Apostles! Here in his second volume Luke shows what the church of Jesus can be.

In the Acts of the Apostles ('Acts' for short) Luke selects events from the first thirty years of the church's life in order to show how the church continued the work which Jesus began. By the end of the book he has sketched the progress of the church's growth as far as Rome.

The first verse of Acts gives the reader a clue: 'In my former book, Theophilus, I wrote about all that Jesus *began* to do and to teach until the day he was taken up to heaven ...' (italics mine).

What he has told us in his Gospel is only half the story. In his earthly life in Palestine Jesus made God real and conveyed his forgiveness, giving people new hope. But now he *continues* as the risen Lord to do the same for people in other places at other times.

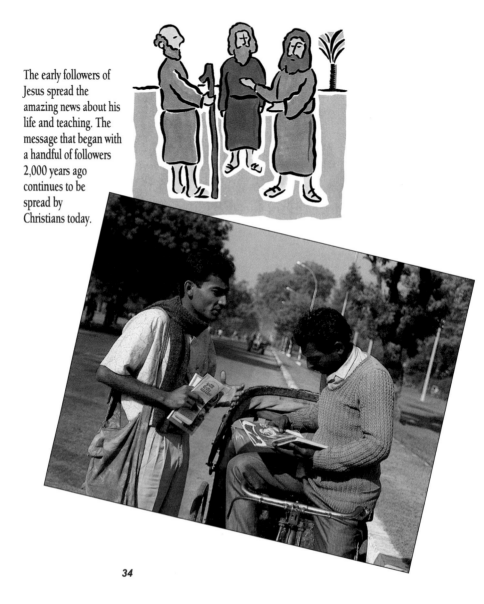

The early followers of Jesus spread the amazing news about his life and teaching. The message that began with a handful of followers 2,000 years ago continues to be spread by Christians today.

How to read the Acts of the Apostles

As with Luke's Gospel, there's a lot to be said for reading the book right through in one or two sittings. You get a sense of the overall shape of Acts if you notice how Luke divides the book up into six sections. Each section ends with a statement summing up 'the story so far', like the summaries in a magazine serial.

For example, the first summary says: 'So the word of God spread. The number of disciples in Jerusalem spread rapidly, and a large number of priests became obedient to the faith.'

This way of setting it out comes from the final words of the risen Jesus recorded in the first chapter of Acts: 'You will receive power when the Holy Spirit comes on you; and you will be my witnesses in Jerusalem, and in all Judea and Samaria, and to the ends of the earth.' Both that promise of Jesus and the shape of Luke's book suggest that his real concern is to tell people what the church is here for and how it has developed.

The book of Acts also introduces one of the great Christian leaders—Paul (whose Hebrew name was Saul), whose dramatic conversion to faith in Jesus Christ was a turning-point in the history of the church.

The six sections in Acts each describe one broad stage in the growth and expansion of the early church:

◆ **Acts 1:1–6:7**
  The earliest church in Jerusalem

◆ **Acts 6:8–9:31**
  The church grows into Samaria and beyond

◆ **Acts 9:32–12:24**
  The first outreach to Gentiles in Palestine and Syria

The news spreads

◆ Acts 12:25–16:5
Paul takes the good news to Cyprus and Asia
Minor (Turkey)

◆ Acts 16:6–19:20
Paul takes the good news into Europe

◆ Acts 19:21–28:31
Paul's mission finally takes him to Rome

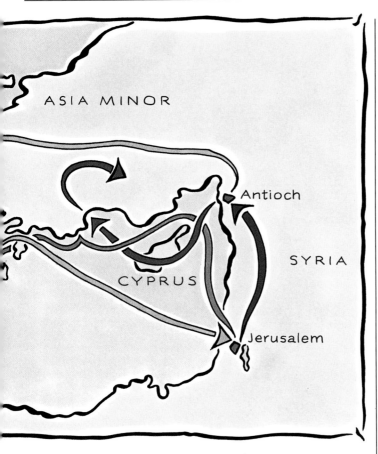

ASIA MINOR

Antioch

SYRIA

CYPRUS

Jerusalem

The message of Acts

In telling how the church grew, Luke wants to emphasize
certain aspects of the story.

Firstly, **the church gets its life from God's Holy
Spirit**. The church is not simply a human
organization, a club for people interested in religion. It
exists because of what happened in Jerusalem at the
festival of Pentecost, seven weeks after Jesus rose from
the dead:

*When the day of Pentecost came, they were all together
in one place. Suddenly a sound like the blowing of*

37

Love in action

Jackie Pullinger, who works among drug addicts in Hong Kong's notorious 'Walled City', tells how she learnt from experience that the church must reflect the mission of Jesus. Christians are to 'be' Jesus to people in need.

I tried to say 'Jesus loves you' in my best Cantonese, and they just said, 'What does that have to do with me?'

So I learnt that it was important not to say the word which nobody could understand. Why would anybody understand 'Jesus loves you' if they don't know who Jesus is and nobody has ever loved them? So I had to be Jesus to them rather than say the words. And that of course would mean things like—

if somebody has no money maybe giving them money,

if they had no food you'd give them yours,

or no house they could sleep in yours.

Or if they had no job it would mean finding them a job,
or visiting them in prison,
or walking an extra mile,
or giving your own clothes,
in fact sharing your life.
That's what I did, and over the years something went in...

Jackie Pullinger, in *The Law of Love*, Otter Productions

Many addicts have been set free from drugs by God's Spirit working through Jackie's team, and have found a new life in Jesus.

a violent wind came from heaven and filled the whole house where they were sitting. They saw what seemed to be tongues of fire that separated and came to rest on each of them. All of them were filled with the Holy Spirit and began to speak in other languages as the Spirit enabled them . . .

ACTS 2:1–4

This dramatic and mysterious account shows how Jesus' followers experienced God's power in a new way, as Jesus had promised them. The rest of chapter 2 shows how this event changed them.

It was the coming of God's Spirit—God's power—which enabled timid people to speak boldly about their faith in Jesus. It made them able to perform miracles of healing. It kept them faithful to Jesus when other people laughed at them or threatened their lives. It made them full of joy and generous concern for others.

And the rest of Acts shows how the church continued to develop because God's Spirit was at work in it.

Secondly, **the life and aims of the church mirror those of Jesus**. The earthly Jesus had a special concern for the poor, for outcasts, for people of different races and for all who were despised in Jewish society. And the church has the same concerns.

Thirdly, **people are brought to faith in Jesus through the preaching of God's message**. There is nothing Luke likes better than summarizing what Peter and Paul preached, and then telling us how those who heard them became followers of Christ.

So in the Acts of the Apostles Luke is telling the story of the early church's growth. By the way he presents the story, he wants to suggest what the church of Jesus should always be like. Christians should depend on God's power. They should reflect the concerns of Jesus. They should share the message of his love.

'You will be my witnesses... to the ends of the earth.' Jesus wants his church to show the same love to others as he did when he was on earth. This is the church's 'mission', to pass on the good news about Jesus.

Letter writing isn't as common today as it once was. In New Testament times it was an important method of long-distance communication. A large part of the New Testament contains letters written by an extraordinary man who became one of the early followers of Jesus. His name was Paul, and his advice to the new churches makes interesting reading.

6

'My love to all of you in Christ Jesus': Paul's letters

● ● ● ● ● ● ● ● ● ● ● ● ●

'I wish I could be with you during the present difficulties. For the moment that is impossible. But I haven't stopped thinking about you. And I am writing my advice in the hope that it may help you until I am able to be with you again...'

You may at some time have begun a letter rather like that. One of the reasons why we write letters is to say to our friends what we would say to them if we could be with them.

The first Christians wrote letters for the same reason. After nearly two thousand years, parts of the apostle Paul's letters are as real and as relevant as when they were first written—to Christians in Turkey, Greece and Rome. And these letters and others by Christian leaders are found after Acts in the New Testament.

Paul was an amazing man by any yardstick. Brought up as a devout Jew, he became a teacher of the Jewish Law and persecuted the followers of Jesus until his dramatic meeting with the risen Christ on the road to Damascus. The story is told in Acts 9, and must have taken place between AD 32 and 35—that is, within about three years of Jesus' resurrection. From then on he became a fearless preacher of his new-found faith.

Many details of his missionary work are not recorded. The missionary journeys recorded in Acts 13–28 cover the period from about AD 46 to about AD 62. In those years of extensive travels, he covered at least 15,000 kilometres. Often he went hungry and thirsty. He faced dangers from bandits. He was imprisoned and flogged by people who hated his message or regarded him as a danger to the state. He was shipwrecked three or four times.

But he started up churches in many of the key cities of Turkey and Greece. As one of the great thinkers of the early church, he enabled new Christians to work out the meaning of Jesus' death and resurrection and to relate their faith to their everyday life. He showed how the life and message of a Palestinian preacher could leap over barriers of race and culture into the cosmopolitan world of Greece and Rome.

Paul's letters were mostly written to churches which he had founded, at places like Corinth, Thessalonica and Philippi. Two of them—the letters to Rome and Colossae—offered teaching and guidance to churches which other people had started. The short letters to Timothy, Titus and Philemon are addressed to individual church leaders.

> The name 'Jesus Christ' was originally 'Jesus the Christ'—Jesus who is God's anointed one. 'Jesus' is in itself a significant name, meaning 'God saves'.

> Paul wrote letters to Christians in churches throughout the Roman Empire. The New Testament preserves Paul's letters to the Romans, Corinthians, Galatians, Ephesians, Philippians, Colossians and Thessalonians, and to individual church leaders: Timothy, Titus and Philemon.

Reading Paul's letters

When you start reading Paul's letters you realize that they are like other letters in several important ways. Most obviously, they are only one end of the correspondence, or conversation, between Paul and a particular church. You are reading someone else's mail, and some of it is explosive stuff!

Sometimes he makes clear that he is responding to an actual letter which the church has written to him (see 1 Corinthians). But we can only guess at what their letter said by reading between the lines of Paul's reply. This can be fun, though sometimes frustrating!

But we can be sure that he didn't write just to pass the time of day. Mostly he wrote to churches because they needed correcting in some way. This is not surprising, because they had all become Christians so recently.

Sometimes he wrote to a church which had misunderstood the essential gospel of Christ. For example, he wrote Galatians because people in the churches in the Roman province of Galatia (in Turkey) believed they could be followers of Jesus only by obeying the whole Jewish Law. On the contrary, Paul insisted, Jesus has won freedom for us by his death and resurrection. We become his people simply by receiving new life from him as a gift.

Sometimes Paul wrote to Christians who were in danger of confusing the truth about Christ with popular ideas from the surrounding world. The church at Colossae—the Colossians—got a letter from him showing how Christ reveals all that we need to know of God.

At other times he wrote to correct distorted ideas about Christian behaviour. The church at Corinth, for instance, was full of people who, in the name of 'Christian liberty', claimed that any kind of behaviour was acceptable to God. So in his second letter to the Corinthians Paul argued that our relationship with Jesus means that we should reflect his character in our lives.

His longest letter, Romans, was probably written partly to persuade Gentile Christians not to despise Jewish believers, whom they now outnumbered. It also gave him the opportunity to set out the message he

Jews expressed their relationship with God by keeping the Law. This included the Ten Commandments which God gave to Moses, as well as other regulations about circumcision and food preparation. Some Jewish Christians thought Gentile Christians could not be truly acceptable to God unless they observed all these regulations.

preached to a church which he had not yet visited. He hoped in this way to gain their support for a planned mission to Spain.

Other letters have more personal motives. In Philippians Paul thanks the Christians at Philippi for the love they have shown by sending him gifts, and he encourages them to stand firm in their faith. The little letter to a Christian called Philemon urges him to act leniently towards a runaway slave.

Whenever we read a New Testament letter we must do a little reading between the lines, asking *why* the situation may have made the writer want to stress these particular truths. This may sound difficult. But a bit of imagination, and discussion among friends, can make it very rewarding.

The important thing to remember is that the letters are not learned theories dreamt up in theologians' studies. They are responses to real people in real situations. They are forged in controversy, bursting with vitality. They are the outpourings of Paul's heart. And Paul was ready to give his life for the sake of the people who found new life through his preaching.

Paul's letters are not theories dreamed up by theologians—they are addressed to real people in real situations.

Every letter is written out of the concern for people with which Paul signs off his letter to Corinth: 'My love to all of you in Christ Jesus.'

Reading the New Testament letters today

Even though the New Testament letters are nearly two thousand years old, some parts of them are easy to understand and to relate to our own lives. For instance, when we read the famous passage about love in 1 Corinthians 13, our difficulty is not in understanding what it means. The main problem lies in living up to its demand.

But other parts of the letters cannot be related so

Bothersome reading

Most people are bothered by those passages in Scripture which they cannot understand; but as for me, I always noticed that the passages in Scripture which troubled me most are those I do understand.

Mark Twain

readily to our own lives. We now live in very different circumstances. Some letters, for example, give guidance about how Christian slaves and slave-owners ought to behave. Such teaching was necessary in a society where slavery was normal and was not going to be abolished in a hurry.

But what do these instructions mean in societies which have at last learnt from the Christian message that slavery degrades humanity? We can't apply them automatically to the modern work-situation in a factory or on a farm because workers aren't slaves. They aren't owned by their employers.

What we can do is to draw *principles* from such teaching which will help our thinking about work and relationships between employer and employee. Ephesians may suggest four principles:

◆ A trustworthy attitude to work is part of our Christian responsibility. We show our commitment to Christ in the workplace as much as anywhere else.

◆ Work is transformed when we recognize that ultimately our responsibility is to Christ rather than to an earthly master. This doesn't mean that repetitive, boring work suddenly becomes exciting. But it can mean that the whole work scene is changed when we relate to our colleagues and employers in the same way as we try to relate to Christ.

◆ All of us—whether slave or master, employee or employer—must give account of our lives to God. Therefore we must aim to work in a way which will please him.

◆ Employers should recognize that their earthly status brings them no special privileges with God. Power carries responsibility. Because they have power to change things, they have a special duty to create a work environment which embodies the belief that people matter more than profit.

Once we have seen what basic principles may be suggested by the New Testament, we can go on to use our God-given minds to work out how the principles might be applied in a particular situation. The New Testament is not like a map giving detailed instructions for every situation we might meet. It is like a compass to point us in the right direction.

Getting started on Paul's letters

Paul's most famous letters are probably Romans and 1 Corinthians. But both letters are quite long. So if you've never read a New Testament letter carefully before, it is a good idea to read a short, more straightforward one first.

Paul's short letter to the Philippians, for example, shows him writing to a church with which he has had a warm relationship for several years. He writes from prison, probably in Rome about AD62, to thank them for a gift of money which has brought great encouragement. In the course of the letter we can learn about prayer, about how God can bring good out of our sufferings, about who Jesus is, about true Christian living, and much else besides.

Other Christian leaders apart from Paul wrote letters which can be found in the New Testament—the letter to

Outline of Philippians

1:1–11   Greetings, thanksgiving and prayer
1:12–26   Paul's imprisonment can't stop the good news
           being heard
1:27–2:18 A plea for unity and Christ-like humility
2:19–30   Paul commends his fellow-workers, Timothy
           and Epaphroditus
3:1–4:1   A warning about false teachers
4:2–9   Paul encourages the Philippians
4:10–20   Thanks for the gift sent by the Philippians
4:21–23   Final greetings

the Hebrews, and letters from James, Peter and John. The variety of issues with which they deal gives some idea of the variety of the first-century churches. Even within fifty years of Jesus' resurrection, church communities were spread far and wide, facing challenges to their beliefs and their lifestyle from many different directions.

The varied nature of these documents helps to ensure that, whatever challenges confront us today, there is a word from the New Testament to guide us.

Whatever challenges us today, the New Testament can show us God's perspective on our situation.

7

Too hot to handle?: the book of Revelation

● ● ● ● ● ● ● ● ● ● ● ● ●

The New Testament's most difficult book comes last, and the difficulty of understanding it has led many Christians to leave it well alone.

Others, making the most of its strange picture-language, have claimed to find in it detailed schemes of the progress of world history towards its end.

But the book of Revelation is not quite so difficult if we take seriously its own clues about its purpose and meaning.

From the opening chapter we notice three things about it:

Firstly, it is a 'revelation from Jesus Christ' about 'what must soon take place'. That word 'revelation' translates the Greek *apokalypsis*, from which we get our words 'apocalypse' and 'apocalyptic'. By giving it this title the author is telling us that his book belongs to the kind of writing known as 'apocalyptic literature'.

There were many examples of Jewish apocalyptic literature. Parts of some Old Testament books—Ezekiel and Daniel, for example—and some New Testament passages, such as Mark 13, have a similar style. It was written when times were bad. People who had experienced intense suffering at the hands of hostile rulers pinned their hope on God creating a new world of justice and peace.

Such literature often gives 'timetables' of God's plans in history which look as though precise predictions are being offered. But the real purpose of these 'predictions' is to suggest that God's purpose *will* triumph in the end,

Outline of Revelation

1:1–20	Prologue: greetings, and John's vision of Christ
2:1–3:22	Messages to the seven churches of Asia
4:1–5:14	A glimpse into heaven, where it is revealed that the saving work of Christ is the key to understanding God's purpose in history
6:1–17, 8:1	The seven seals: a symbolic description of events leading up to the final coming of Christ
7:1–17	First interlude: the church is secure in God's care
8:2—9:21, 11:15–19	The seven trumpets: a further symbolic description of events leading up to the final coming of Christ
10:1–11:14	Second interlude: the church's task, to witness in the face of suffering
12:1–14:20	Third interlude: conflict between the church and evil powers
15:1–16:21	The seven bowls of God's wrath: a further symbolic description of events leading up to the final coming of Christ
17:1–19:10	The fall of 'Babylon': Rome's anti-Christian empire falls prey to its own forces of destruction
19:11–21	Christ's final coming
20:1–10	The reign of Christ and the destruction of Satan
20:11–15	The final judgment
21:1–22:5	The new heaven and the new earth
22:6–21	Epilogue: concluding promises and warnings

not to tell us exactly *when* it will happen.

Apocalypses also enjoy using picture-language which is strange to us—beasts, dragons, plagues, for example. These symbols would be no more strange to the readers of Revelation than football and Coca-Cola are to us.

It may involve us in some effort to find out what the symbols mean. But if we look at other writings from the New Testament period the meanings are there to be discovered. The fault in many modern interpretations of Revelation is that they *impose* a meaning on the picture-language of the book without troubling to ask what it would have meant to the book's first readers, in the context of first-century Christianity.

Secondly, this book is also prophecy. Like Old Testament prophets, the author of this book speaks God's word to particular situations. He expresses God's warnings of judgment and promises of deliverance. We can see this most clearly in chapters 2 and 3, which contain messages to seven churches. These messages look very like some Old Testament prophetic statements, with their warnings and encouragements.

Thirdly, Revelation is also a letter. The author uses the same kind of opening greeting which can be found in other New Testament letters (see Philippians). He identifies himself as John. It is often assumed that this is the apostle John, one of Jesus' original twelve followers. But he doesn't call himself an apostle, and may be someone else of the same name.

His readers are 'the seven churches in the province of Asia', in what we now call Western Turkey. Like any letter writer, John expects his letter to be understood by its first readers. And he has their particular circumstances in mind. He is not writing coded messages for future generations, but challenging his readers and warning them in the light of persecution which he sees coming their way.

Many of the early Christians were sentenced to death by the Roman authorities for following Jesus. In parts of the world today, Christians are persecuted because of their faith. The last book of the Bible contains a powerful message of hope for all who are oppressed or in danger.

Revelation for today

When Christians in stable and tolerant democracies neglect the book of Revelation, they are showing a lack of sympathy for their brothers and sisters who face persecution for their faith. This book has always 'come alive' for Christians who find themselves in danger similar to the oppression by the Roman authorities which threatened John's first readers.

John was probably writing during the reign of the emperor Domitian (AD 81–96). When Domitian issued a decree demanding to be called 'Lord and God', Christians' loyalty to Christ as the one Lord made them unable to submit to this absolute demand.

As persecution threatened, they would be asking, 'Where is God in all this? Does power really lie in God's hands, or in Domitian's?' John responds by showing them a Christ who was himself 'the faithful witness' in the face of suffering and is now 'the ruler of the kings of the earth'.

To Christians fearful for the future this Christ declares, 'Do not be afraid. I am the First and the Last. I am the Living One; I was dead, and behold I am alive for ever and ever!'

Christ has gone through suffering before us, and goes through suffering with us now.

John points his readers to the Christ who has gone through suffering before them, and goes through their sufferings with them now. His victory over death is the guarantee that in the end God's purpose will triumph. Christ will come again one day to bring the course of history to its end. He will welcome his people into the 'new heaven and new earth' which is his destiny for them.

In encouraging his readers to face suffering, John is writing out of his own experience. He himself has suffered exile to the island of Patmos because of his Christian witness. And what he writes is not the ramblings of his mind, but a vision given to him by the risen Christ.

We may never understand all the details. But there remains much that we can gain from it, if we keep asking it the right questions:

◆ **What comfort does it offer to Christians threatened by persecution?**

◆ **What challenge does it offer Christians to maintain a distinctive lifestyle despite the pressures to conform to the surrounding society?**

◆ **What warnings does it give to a godless world?**

◆ **What does it say about the task of the church in the face of conflict?**

◆ **How does our ultimate hope of eternal life influence our attitude to life now?**

A message for today

● ● ● ● ● ● ● ● ● ● ● ● ●

We have explored how the New Testament books came to be written. We have thought about the message they contain. But the question remains: why should such old books influence people's lives today?

Why should we take notice of them? How can they guide our lives when our world is so different from the world of the first Christians?

Certainly most people's experience of the world is very different from that of first-century people. The development of science and medicine, travel and education has raised for us questions of which the first Christians knew nothing.

We face moral questions about abortion and about Aids. We have the ability to devastate the world in an instant through nuclear weapons, or more slowly through pollution of the environment. We are in desperate need of guidance in such matters. But the Bible says nothing directly about them.

Why do people still read the New Testament now? Because it answers the questions and addresses the needs of people of every age and culture.

The Bible speaks today

Yet Christians still find no book is so life-giving, so indispensable as the Bible. Why is this? There are several reasons why it continues to speak across the centuries.

Though the world has changed in many ways, some things have changed very little since New Testament times. Human nature does not change. We are still the same bundles of hopes and fears, of guilt and generosity, of self-seeking and self-giving, as the people whom Jesus and Luke and Paul met. We have the same basic needs and the same questions about life as they did.

We need a purpose for life that is more than material comfort. We wonder what lies beyond death. Millions are gripped by the fear of fate and the power of astrology, just as the Greek readers of Paul's letters were. We wonder how people of different races and social classes can live in harmony, and we can find new hope just as first-century Christians did when they saw God breaking down barriers between Jews and Gentiles, rich and poor, slaves and free people. We know the power of evil and the need of forgiveness.

So it is no surprise that people in many cultures speak of the Bible not only as a book which they read, but as the book which reads them.

In actual experience people all over the world constantly find that the New Testament speaks to them in a vital, up-to-date way. When you think about it, it's quite extraordinary how this small book, written in the cultures of ancient Palestine, Greece and Rome, should communicate today to people in every culture under the sun.

The Bible is able to speak to people in all the varied situations of life because, as Christians believe, it is 'inspired' by God. Although it is a human book, produced through the normal processes of writing, it is also a divine book.

When Luke wrote his Gospel, as we have seen, he did research to establish the facts as any other historian

Some things have changed very little since New Testament times—human nature never changes.

might have done. When Paul wrote his letters, he responded to questions raised by his churches as any other concerned pastor might have done. That is the human aspect of their writing.

But because Luke was recording the life and words of Jesus, and because Paul was called personally to be Christ's apostle, there is a special sense in which they are giving us God's word. That is the divine aspect of their writing.

Paul's second letter to Timothy makes this claim:

All Scripture is God-breathed and is useful for teaching, rebuking, correcting and training in righteousness, so that the man of God may be thoroughly equipped for every good work.

2 TIMOTHY 3:16

A changed heart

A village tyrant in Sri Lanka ruled his neighbourhood with an iron fist. Amaradasa had become rich from illegal brewing and killing cattle for beef. One woman after another was bullied into sharing his home. The whole village lived in fear of him.

His friend had been given a booklet which presented the Bible's teaching on various themes. As he read what it said about forgiveness he found new hope for himself and thought, 'This is certainly good news for me. But even more for my friend.'

The man gave the booklet to Amaradasa, who read and re-read it. At first he was tense, bitter. Then slowly he relaxed and began to smile. From that moment his friend noticed a change, which could only be the work of God in his life.

At first Amaradasa wanted to honour the miraculous message, so he fixed the paper on the wall of his house and began to worship it. But he found no peace in his heart. Finally, he wrote to the Bible Society which had produced the booklet, asking for help. Six months later, he was at the centre of a young and growing church, serving the village he had terrorized.

He is referring to the Old Testament here, since at the time of writing the New Testament had not been brought together as a collection of books. But it is reasonable to think that the God who inspired the Old Testament would also give us documents which show the fulfilment of its promises in the coming of Jesus.

The books of the New Testament, written as they were by the apostles or by people who were very close to them, are the earliest witness to Jesus that exists. They are the closest we can get to his life and to the first impact of his death and resurrection. No other Christian documents are so early or so full of first-hand testimony.

It is impossible to *prove* that the Bible is specially inspired by God. It is a matter of faith—and of personal experience. For down through the centuries Christians have found that through its pages they meet with God and come into an experience of his love. By it they are challenged, guided and kept in Christ's way.

9

A message for me

● ● ● ● ● ● ● ● ● ● ● ● ● ●

Understanding the message of the New
Testament is one thing. Acting on it is
another.

Big claims are made for its influence on
people now, though it describes events of two
thousand years ago. But how exactly does it
speak to our lives? And what should our
response be?

We might think of the New Testament as speaking to us
in three ways:

Firstly, it speaks about **our relationship with God**. For
instance, the teaching of Jesus in the Gospels and parts
of the New Testament letters tell us what God is like.
Stories in the Gospels about people meeting Jesus show
how we can come to him to find forgiveness, healing and
new life. Teaching in the letters shows how our
relationship with him can grow through our experience
of God's Spirit in us and our obedience to his guidance.

Secondly, it speaks about **our relationship to God's
people, the church**. The books of the Bible were written
mainly for a community, not for individuals. It's
important—especially for people who do not enjoy
reading on their own—to realize that the natural context

for learning what the Bible says and means is a group of Christians. This might be a large group listening together to a sermon which explains a Bible passage. Or a small group of people discussing it, arguing about it, struggling to work out its meaning for their lives together.

This is how most Christians grow towards maturity in their faith. This is how God shows the world that he is real and active—as a group of Christians learn from the New Testament how to live in Christ-like love towards each other and towards the rest of society.

Thirdly, it speaks about **our relationship to society and to the world**. It shows us a God who cares about the world he has made, who longs that men and women should come to know his love and should care for each other. And it shows how Christians are meant to reflect in their own lives God's character and his concern for the world. It is full of examples of what it means in particular circumstances to 'love the Lord your God... and your neighbour as yourself'.

The New Testament will not give us ready-made answers about how to respond to dilemmas in the modern world which were unknown to the biblical writers. It isn't a cook-book with a detailed recipe for every modern situation. It doesn't treat us as children needing to be told exactly what to do all the time.

Instead, the Bible's message gradually makes us the people we are meant to be—people of love and insight, able to think wisely and responsibly about God's will for the present. **The Bible makes the Christian, and the Christian responds to situations in a Christ-like way.**

Taking the Bible's message seriously gradually changes Christians into the people God made them to be.

Having the right approach

If we are to come close to God and to benefit from reading the Bible, it's important to approach it with a

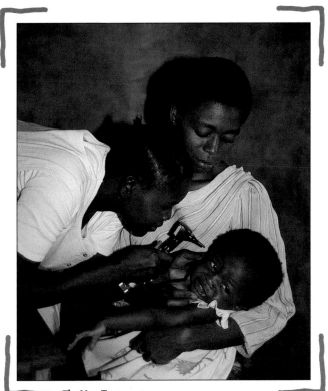

The New Testament
clearly shows that
caring for one another
and putting the needs
of others before our
own are essential parts
of the Christian life.

healthy attitude. I suggest the following guidelines:

◆ **Have an attitude of listening to God. Expect him to speak to you—to teach, challenge and encourage you through the words of the Bible.**

◆ **Pray for the Holy Spirit's guidance. Because the Bible was inspired by God, God's Spirit will help us to understand and apply it to our lives.**

◆ **Expect to learn from the experiences of other Christians as you study the Bible with them. Because of who they are and what they've been through, they will notice things in a passage which haven't occurred to you. And you will have insights to share with them.**

◆ **Ask God to show you what action your study should lead to. Then he will gradually change you, and will change the world through you and others like you. But Bible study is of no value unless it leads to action. Jesus said:**

I will show you what he is like who comes to me and hears my words and puts them into practice. He is like a man building a house, who dug deep down and laid the foundation on rock. When the flood came, the torrent struck that house but could not shake it, because it was well built. But the one who hears my words and does not put them into practice is like a man who built a house on the ground without a foundation. The moment the torrent struck that house, it collapsed and its destruction was complete.

LUKE 6:47–49

Ask and it will be given to you;
seek and you will find; knock
and the door will be opened to you.
For everyone who asks receives;
he who seeks finds; and to him who
knocks, the door will be opened.

JESUS' WORDS RECORDED IN MATTHEW 7:7–8

Come near to God and he will come
near to you.

JAMES 4:8

Whoever comes to me I will never
drive away.

JESUS' WORDS RECORDED IN JOHN 6:37

Picture acknowledgments

Illustrations and maps by Tony de Saulles

Photographs by Ebenezer Pictures (Susanna Burton) 55, (James Heard) 34, (C and J Pemberton) 61; Lion Publishing (David Alexander) 17, (David Townsend) 26; Telegraph Colour Library 51; ZEFA 6